A+
books

Know Your Emotions

Sad Is...

by Cheyenne Nichols

CAPSTONE PRESS
a capstone imprint

2

Sad's that gloomy feeling
when you wish for something new.
You do not feel like laughing
and your world seems glum and blue.

3

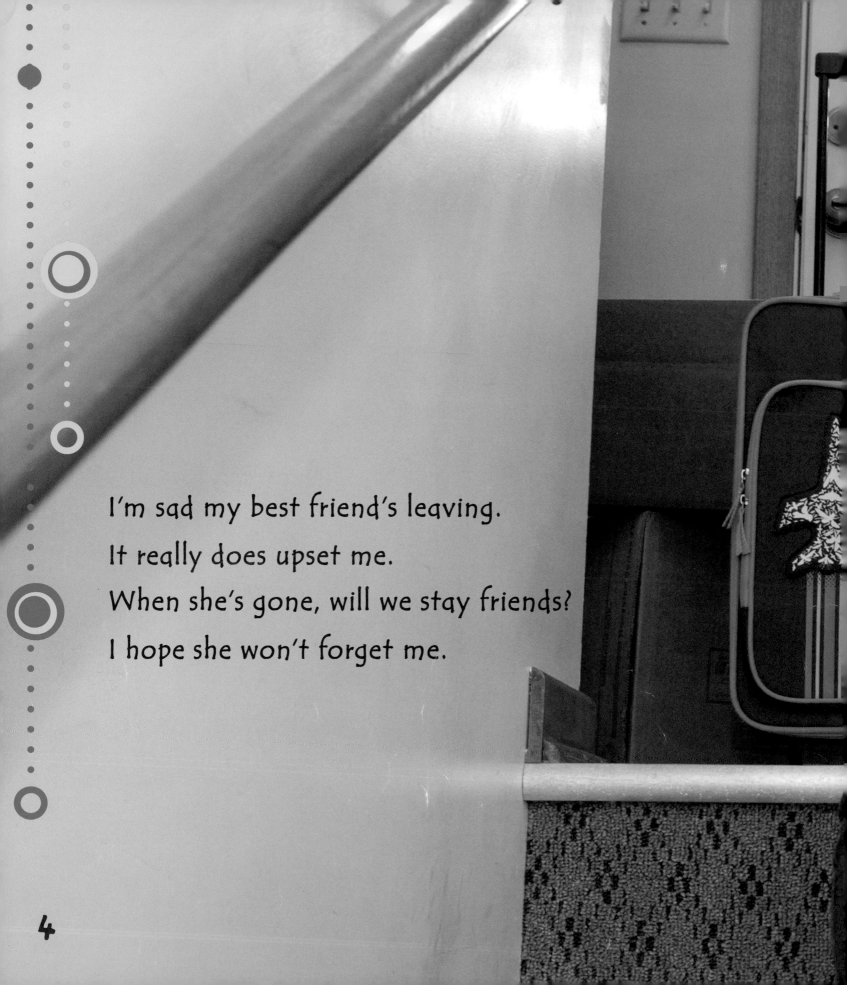

I'm sad my best friend's leaving.
It really does upset me.
When she's gone, will we stay friends?
I hope she won't forget me.

4

We double-dribbled. Then we fouled.
We hardly scored, and that was tough.
My eyes are wet and stinging now—
To lose a game is really rough.

My brother races fire trucks.
My sister cartwheels by.
I'm stuck in bed because I'm sick—
and I just want to cry.

10

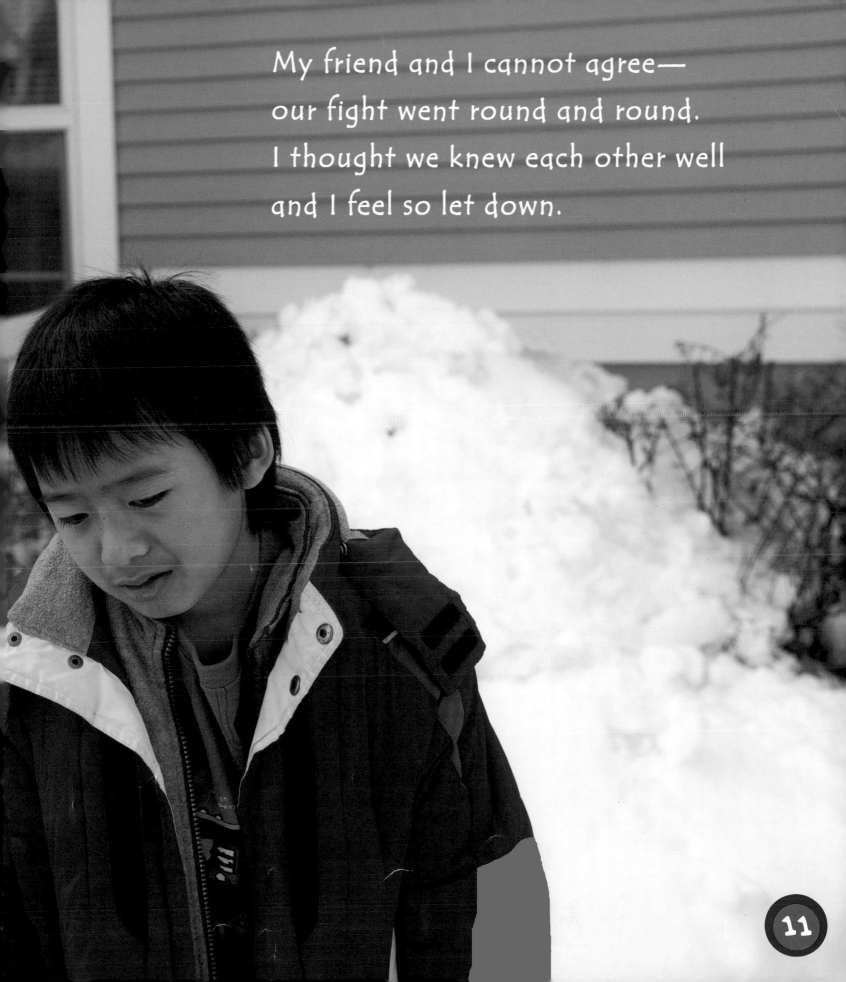

My friend and I cannot agree—
our fight went round and round.
I thought we knew each other well
and I feel so let down.

11

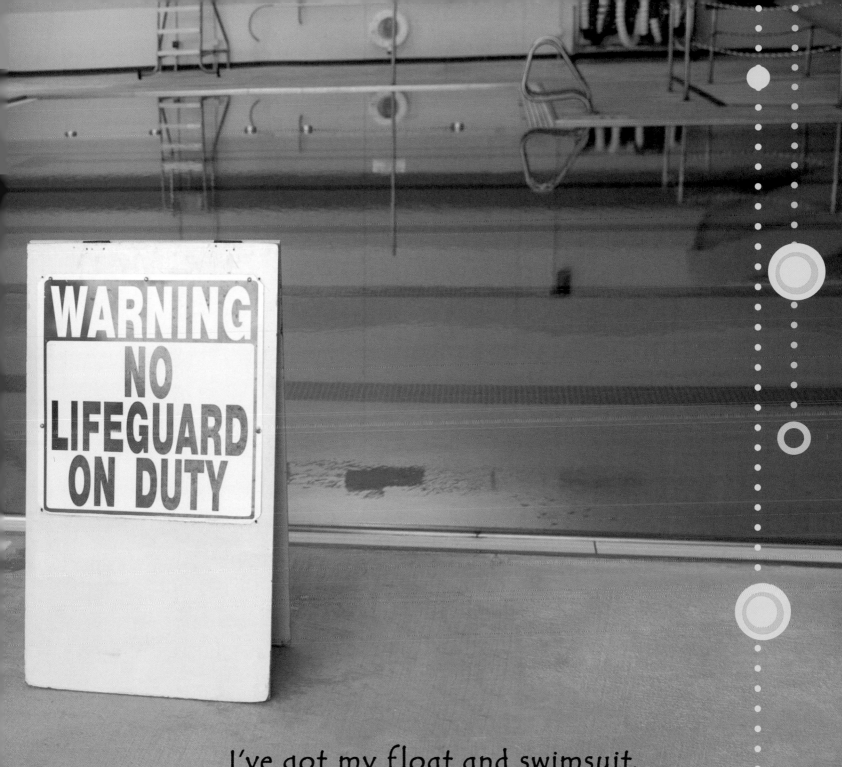

I've got my float and swimsuit.
My goggles are brand new.
But the pool is sad and empty
And that's how I feel too.

14

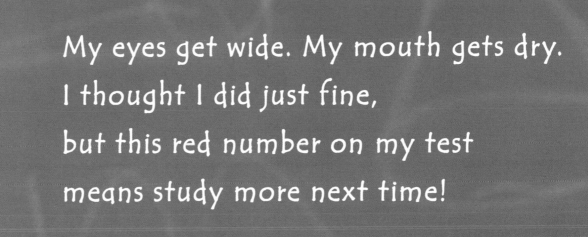

My eyes get wide. My mouth gets dry.
I thought I did just fine,
but this red number on my test
means study more next time!

When you say you are leaving,
I hold on tight to you.
I wish that we were stuck this way
with super-magic-glue.

Of course it's just a movie,
but my eyes don't seem to know
if it's real or make believe—
my tears well up and flow.

19

When sad is sticking to me,
When I wear it like a sweater,
I just relax and tell myself:
Tomorrow will be better.

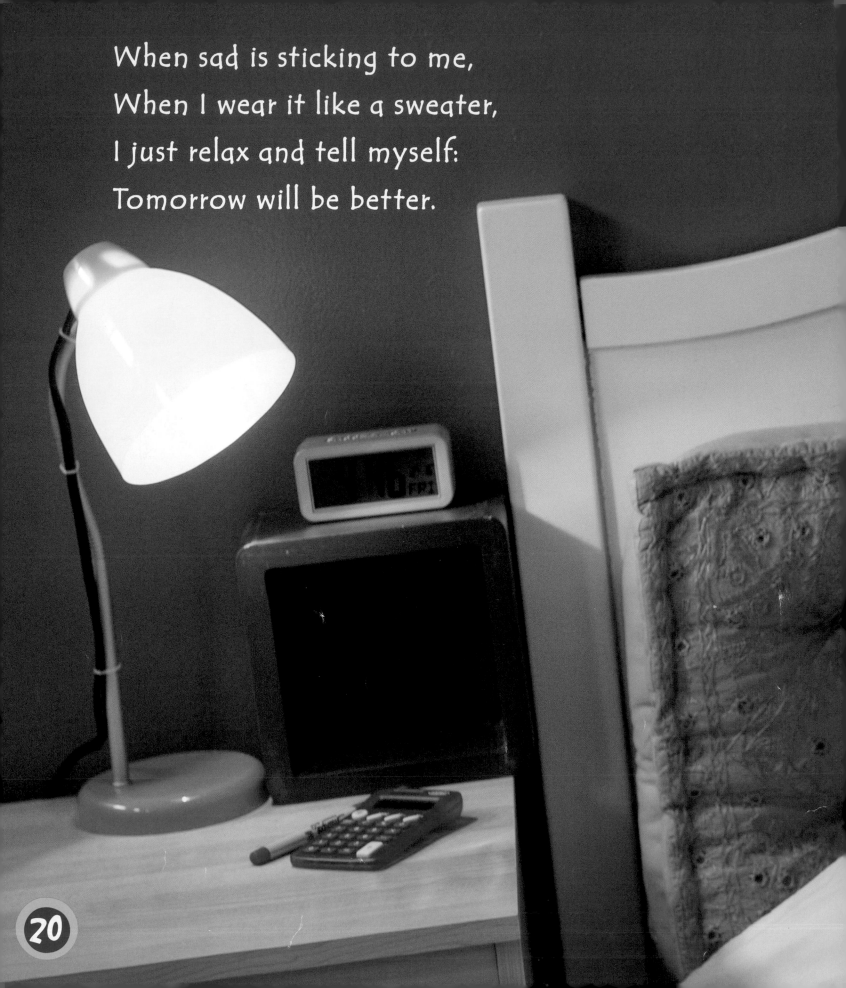

21

Glossary

gloomy—dark and sad

glum—sad

sting—a hot, sharp pain

well—to rise to the surface and usually flow forth

Read More

Aboff, Marcie. *Everyone Feels Sad Sometimes*. Everyone Has Feelings. Minneapolis: Picture Window Books, 2010.

Bingham, Jane. *Everybody Feels Sad*. Everybody Feels … New York: Crabtree Pub. Co., 2008.

Medina, Sarah. *Sad*. Feelings. Chicago: Heinemann Library, 2007.

INTERNET SITES

FactHound offers a safe, fun way to find Internet sites related to this book. All of the sites on FactHound have been researched by our staff.

Here's all you do:

Visit *www.facthound.com*

Type in this code: 9781429660433

Super-cool stuff! Check out projects, games and lots more at **www.capstonekids.com**

INDEX

A+ Books are published by Capstone Press,
151 Good Counsel Drive, P.O. Box 669, Mankato, Minnesota 56002.
www.capstonepub.com

Books published by Capstone Press are manufactured with paper
containing at least 10 percent post-consumer waste.

Library of Congress Cataloging-in-Publication Data
Nichols, Cheyenne.
  Sad is... / by Cheyenne Nichols.
     p. cm.—(A+ books. Know your emotions)
  Includes bibliographical references and index.
  Summary: "Photographs and short rhyming verses describe how it feels to be sad"—Provided by publisher.
  ISBN 978-1-4296-6043-3 (library binding) ISBN 978-1-4296-7052-4 (paperback)
  1. Sadness in children—Juvenile literature. 2. Sadness—Juvenile literature. 3. Emotions in children—Juvenile
literature. I. Title. II. Series.
  BF723.S15S25 2011
  152.4—dc22   2011006127

Credits

Jeni Wittrock, editor; Alison Thiele, designer; Svetlana Zhurkin, media researcher; Sarah Schuette, photo stylist;
     Marcy Morin, photo scheduler; Eric Manske, production specialist

Photo Credits

Capstone Studio/Karon Dubke, all interior photographs
iStockphoto/wayra, cover

Note to Parents, Teachers, and Librarians

The Know Your Emotions series uses full color photographs and a nonfiction format to introduce the concept of emotions.
Sad Is ... is designed to be read aloud to a pre-reader or to be read independently by an early reader. Photographs help
listeners and early readers understand the text and concepts discussed. The book encourages further learning by including
the following sections: Glossary, Read More, Internet Sites, Index. Early readers may need assistance using these features.

Printed in the United States of America in North Mankato, Minnesota.
032011   006110CGF11